simple
RULES

... in building, art & life ...

BOOK
Nº 1

Simplicity is the heart of elegant proportion

SHANNON TAYLOR SCARLETT

Simple Rules

Published by Shannon Taylor Scarlett, Architects
Eleven Pine Tree Road, Wellesley MA 02482

ISBN-13: 978-1484152072
ISBN-10: 1484152077

Simple Rules is a new kind of builder handbook/design guide.

Inspired by long forgotten sources, the design content included here—timeless composition principles, elegant proportional systems, building techniques and formulas for making buildings more beautiful—is intended as a guide for the modern builder who cares about aesthetics and meaning as much or more than the bottom line.

In this small guide a few select concepts and techniques, salvaged mostly from 18th, 19th and early 20th century builder pocket references and architectural guides, have been resurrected and abridged—or interpreted where possible—for practical use by the 21st century architect and homebuilder.

Simple building practices like the traditional design principles and conventions included here were used in the past to make places that were at once familiar and meaningful, sensible and beautiful. While there is a focus on American vernacular building traditions, most of the ideas here are universal. The design concepts are equally applicable to modern design. In fact, they are intended to serve as archetypes for a new modern architecture, to free builders from the need to simply replicate old styles.

Revealing and instructive for homeowners as well, this collection of rules and traditions should prove handy to anyone involved in residential design, home construction, finance or purchase; inspiring to artists and craftsmen; and appealing to the armchair architect, and others who simply enjoy thoughtfully designed homes.

Shannon Taylor Scarlett, Architect
March 2014

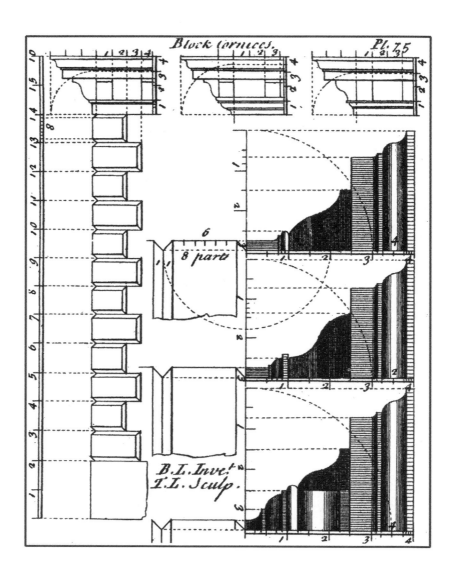

Block cornices.

Pl. 75

8 part

B.L. Invet.
T.L. Sculp.

4

Table of Contents

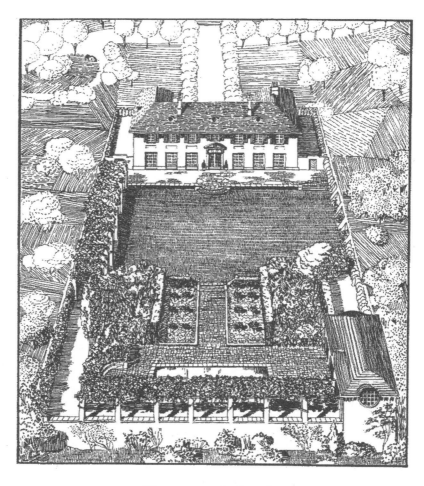

House and Garden

(Note: All illustrations have been copied from old books, trade journals and design guidelines. Most images were created a hundred years or more ago; and some are copies or reinterpretations of much earlier architecture.)

Introduction

Like the 1896 guide, *Modern Carpentry and Building,* "This book is intended as an aid to the workman, a veritable handy book to be carried in his coat pocket or in his box of tools, ready for instant reference, not left at home."

The contents differ for the modern user only in familiarity, as these foundational design principles regarding aesthetics, symbolism and meaning of place were for the old-timer carpenter, simply routine. Unfortunately, these principles began to lose their footing in the late 1800s, when building practices shifted toward more commercial technologies. Today this design wisdom is inaccessible to the average homebuilder; even architects would do well to study these rules.

Handbooks illustrating what was once common knowledge pertaining to design aesthetics, balance and rules of composition—aesthetic qualities Talbot Hamlin described in *The Enjoyment of Architecture*—eventually became overshadowed by charts, formulas, and practices geared toward new materials, and economical building systems:

"The dominant qualities that are common to all beautiful and unified buildings [are] so uniform that they have been codified into laws, or perhaps more really, rules of artistic composition. If they are once understood and applied, sound criticism is the inevitable result, so it is necessary that they be carefully considered.

They are, in brief, the laws of balance, rhythm, good proportion, climax (centre of interest), and harmony... these laws or rules, deduced from good buildings, are practically the same as the laws that govern good literature or good music; that seems sufficient commentary upon their validity."

The aim of this book is to remind everyone in the building community that simple beauty and meaning—traits common to most old buildings—is still reproducible in new homes, and that many traditional building techniques are still applicable in today's economy, and within current construction practices.

Learning the principles underlying the design and construction of those old buildings does require a time investment, but the effort pays off once the rules that focus on quality become internalized and routine. These rules—united with the functionality, building materials and details relevant to modern life—help make good design simple.

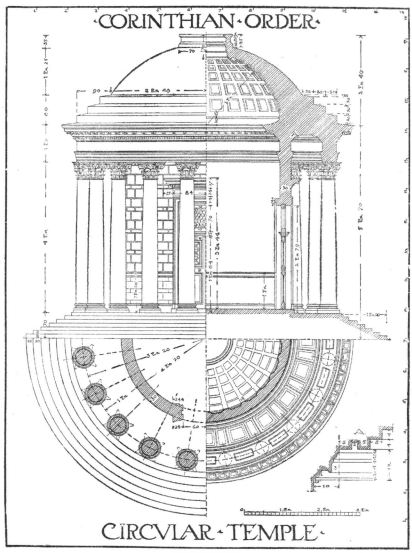

simple

RULE

1

STRENGTH, UTILITY, BEAUTY

"All architecture should possess strength, utility, and beauty."

~ Vitruvius

Vitruvius Pollio, Marcus (c80 BC- c15 BC) wrote *De Architectura,* the first and most famous treatises on architecture. Based on Greek architecture, the ten books codified the theories guiding Roman architecture of his time. He described a geometric relationship between nature, architecture and the body of man, which was the basis of the famous DaVinci drawing of the Renaissance man inscribed in a circle and square.

STRENGTH, UTILITY, BEAUTY

Strength arises from

carrying down the foundations to a good solid bottom, and from making a proper choice of materials without parsimony†

Utility arises from a

judicious distribution of the parts, so that their purposes be duly answered, and that each have its proper situation

Beauty is produced by

the pleasing appearance and good taste of the whole, and by the **dimensions of all the parts being duly proportioned to each other**

† parsimony: economy of means, cost-cutting

~Marcus Vitruvius Pollio
De Architectura, Book

·FRONT·ELEVATION·

"As one principal figure
should always stand out as
the foremost, ...to which
all subordinate purposes
should contribute and lend
their aid. "

ONE MAIN DESIGN

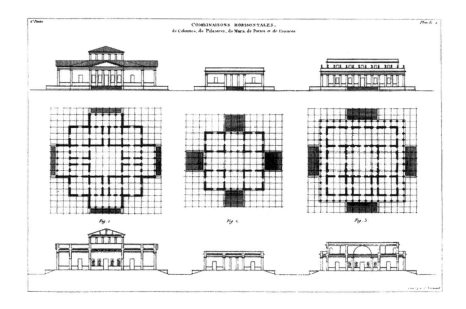

Jean-Nicolas-Louis Durand
Recueil et parallele des edifices de tout genre (1801)

Durand explored—with his diagrams of known buildings all drawn at
the same scale—the concept of typology, looking for common
structural types and forms

Durand, Jean-Nicolas-Louis (1760 –1834) was a French architect, author and
instructor of rational design through typology. He developed a Neoclassical
system of architectural design that employed simple modular elements, that
was viewed as a sign of the industrialized building components of the future.

simple
RULE

2

ONE MAIN DESIGN

"One main design should ever be obvious, to which all subordinate purposes should contribute."

~ George Harris

Harris, George, (1809-1890) English barrister and judge with strong interests in anthropology, architecture and psychology published a two-volume treatise titled *A Philosophical Treatise on the Nature and Constitution of Man.* Many theories were novel, but he also utilized medieval principles and terminology.

ONE MAIN DESIGN

If the attention of the mind is divided, the perception is confused, and the impression much weakened. Hence, the *union together of the different parts of a composition is an essential principle...*

It is, indeed, alone by this means, that all the various figures and groups become amalgamated into one whole; that they are made in reality to constitute a composition, instead of remaining independent objects.

"In every composition the entire design should appear to be directed to one object, to proceed from one mind, and to be of the same character."

~ George Harris
The Theory of the Arts: or, Art in Relation to Nature

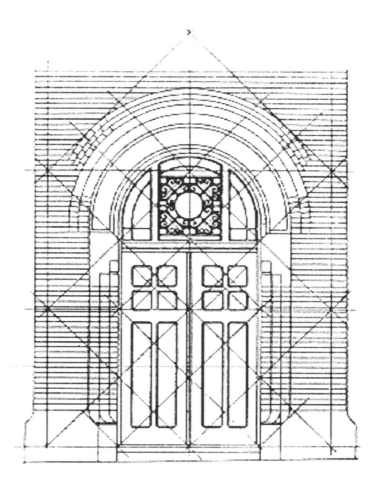

"… the general vigour and impressiveness of the entire piece, is produced by the concentration together into one composition of a variety of different objects and circumstances which all tend to the same result…"

simple
RULE

3

PARTS ADAPTED TO WHOLE

"Each part of a complete
composition fits and adapts itself
to the rest; and each is essential
for the completion of the whole."

~ George Harris

PARTS ADAPTED TO WHOLE

"Parts in a composition should bear the same relation to one another, and to the principal figure or individual in it, as the different members of the same body, although varying extensively in their nature and purposes, and exercising very different functions one from the other, bear to one another, and especially to the head.

Although these several parts of the composition may be all actually disconnected, they are all related to each other. ... Like the different creations in nature, all bear their respective and appropriate parts in the same grand system..."

The Decoration of a Commonplace Room

The Theory of the Arts: or, Art in Relation to Nature, Volume 2
~ George Harris

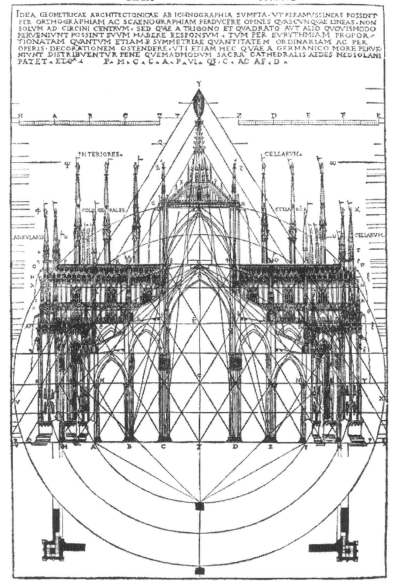

Dutch village town center, rooflines, building widths, gable details and crenellations, window type and spacing consistent

simple
RULE
4

GENIUS OF THE PLACE

"Consult the genius of the place in all."

~ Alexander Pope

Pope, Alexander (1688 –1744) know for his Augustan poetry, Pope used similar principles as an inspiration for landscape design. He established the *genius loci* an important principle in garden and landscape design, which later influenced architects as well.

Photo credit Colin Brough, SXC

cityscape views of south Edinburgh, Scotland, rooflines, building material, dormers, window type and building spacing are consistent

"It is no uncommon error to design a street facade wholly regardless of this consideration. We too often see, in the midst of the irregularity of ordinary street architecture, an elevation with its centre and wings, a pediment here and a projection there, the whole presenting a complex composition all crowded into a small compass, producing painful confusion instead of that repose which, amidst such discrepancies of form and fashion, the distracted eye so much desires to dwell upon; and this is often done to the serious disparagement of the building itself, by detracting from its individual importance."

GENIUS OF THE PLACE

*California suburban town center, arches, rooflines, building heights,
window type and spacing consistent*

"This *genius loci*—the local circumstances of the spot—should not fail to have its due weight in the selection of style and character.

...in the streets of a city, some uniformity of outline seems preferable to that endless miscellany of houses of varied heights, shapes, and sizes, which make some of our large streets so preeminently ugly." ~ Mr. Smirke's Lectures

Smirke, Sydney (1798 – 1877) London architect, and lecturer, received the RIBA Royal Gold Medal in 1860

HAROLD KENNARD, ARCHITECT

equal distribution of detail and composition front and side, same roof form repeated, smaller side porch compliments front porch

simple
RULE
5

THREE DIMENSIONALITY

"Always keep in mind the
perspective appearance when
designing the exterior of a
detached building, and not merely
the front elevation."

~ Richard Brown, Architect

Brown, Richard, Architect *(1800s)* English architect, author of domestic
architectural pattern books

THREE DIMENSIONALITY

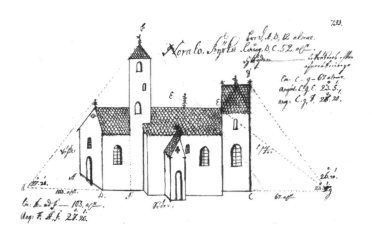

"…imagine the building as it appears to a person walking all around it… From every possible view a really good building must have balance, and this accounts for the comparative failure of some of our informal American country houses.

They seem manifestly to be designed with one view point, or two, in mind; from these points they are good, perfect in balance and composition, but from other points the same buildings are a mere hodge-podge, and they lack that little accent on the centre of balance given by a chimney or flower box, or some little point of interest, that would have made the whole seem balanced and in repose."

~ Talbot Hamlin
The Enjoyment of Architecture

*side view is the first perspective seen as approached from the road,
porch entered both from sides and front*

"From every possible view
a really good building must
have balance..."
~ Talbot Hamlin

(2+1)

5
(3+2)

3

3

3(2+1)

3

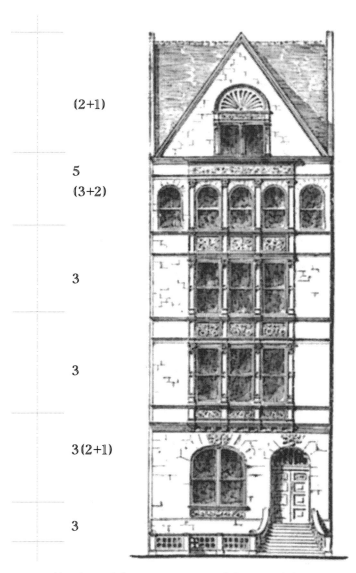

application of the composition of three and five parts

simple
RULE
6

DIVISION IN 3 OR 5 PARTS

"simplicity, in the disposition of a great variety, is best accomplished by following nature's constant rule, of dividing composition into three or five parts, or parcels"

~ Hogarth

Hogarth, William (1697 –1764) was an English painter, printmaker, pictorial satirist, social critic, and editorial cartoonist credited with pioneering western sequential art. He published his ideas of artistic design in his book *The Analysis of Beauty*, where he professed to define the principles of beauty and grace.

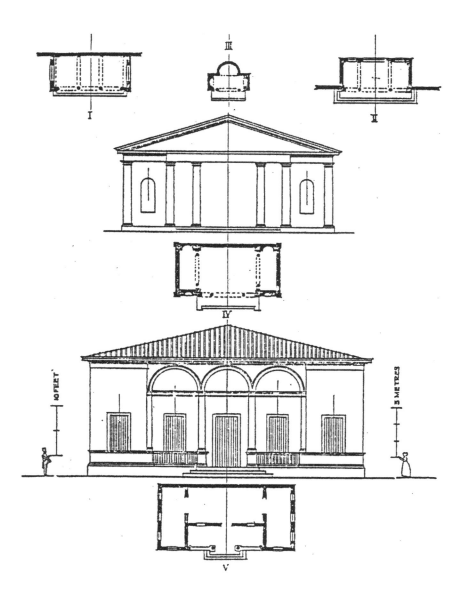

3 and 5 part Loggias
Elements of Form & Design in Classic Architecture

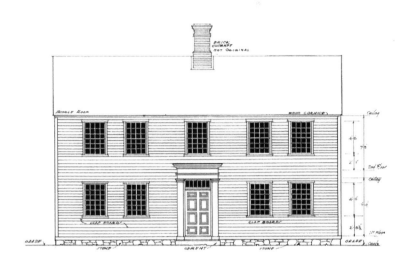

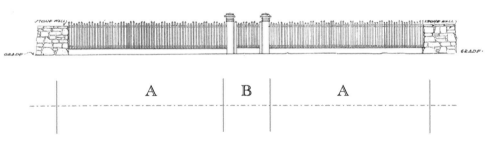

"three objects, the center one of which is emphasized, have great compelling power in artistic expression." Hogarth

*small fireplace becomes focal point of the room when benches are
built-in either side to create an inglenook*

simple
RULE
7

FOCAL POINTS

"The climax must be the most interesting motive of the composition."

~ John Vredenburgh Van Pelt

Van Pelt, John Vredenburgh (1874 – 1962) was an architectural historian, author, and American architect active in early to mid-twentieth-century New York City.

FOCAL POINTS

Six Laws of Composition

1. The interest must be focalized, and have its most *potent* expression in one point. ...the climax.

2. The number of secondary focal points must be reduced to minimum; ...and those, conceived primarily in regard to the climax and in their *comparative importance*, must work up to it.

3. Of the different minor elements ...each relating to its own especial focal point, must still feel the *influence* of the climax.

4. Different elements must balance in such a manner that the average of interest will fall in the middle of the frame... balance in relation to the *center of gravity* must be observed.

5. That the different elements of a composition ...may attain to the highest interest, they must *contrast* one with the other.

6. That unity exist in the composition, the laws of harmony must be observed; and *no foreign element* introduced.

~ John Vredenburgh Van Pelt
A Discussion of Composition, Especially as Applied to Architecture

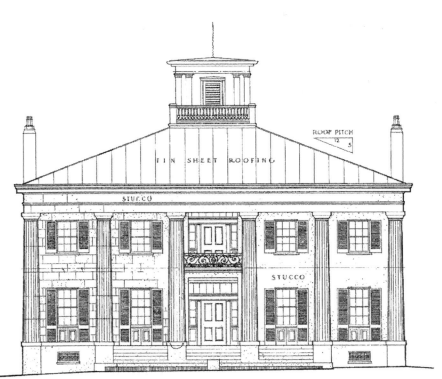

·North Elevation 4

FIG. 9.— HOUSE AT BEAUVAIS, c. 1540.
Good example of the French Renaissance in its simpler manifestations.

character, direction or relative position of the parts are mostly uniform

simple
RULE

8

UNIFORMITY

"The law of uniformity applies in nature and design where the character, direction or relative position of the parts are mostly uniform."

~ John Addington Symonds

Symonds, John Addington (1840 –1893) was an English poet, and literary critic, he was known for his cultural history of the Italian Renaissance. Wrote *The Principles of Beauty*.

DESIGN FOR FOUR ROOM COTTAGE OF FRAME CONSTRUCTION

one side corresponding to the other without strict symmetrical balance

"Even where variety of lines and forms is most natural, ...the arrangement is most agreeable to the eye, when, without formality, there is a certain degree of symmetry, as when one side... corresponds to the other, without conspicuously balancing it... where there is the greatest apparent diversity, it is easy to trace the law of uniformity."

UNIFORMITY

snowflake geometry

a law of nature

"In foliage there is not only the general likeness of the leaves and branches, but the direction or the relative position of the leaves is in a great measure uniform, and a departure from it produces an impression of confusion or discomposure which may even cause us to attribute unhealthiness to the plant or tree in which we observe this derangement."

wisteria on pergola

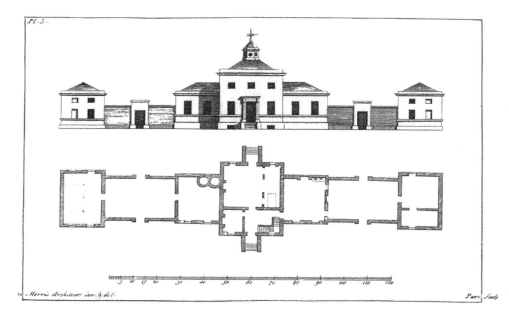

Palladian style villa by Robertus Morris, Architect

"The simpler schemes are the most universally successful, and it becomes increasingly difficult to manage the whole composition as motives are added, since the increasing complexity makes it difficult for the eye to seize at once the inherent balance, which is such a large element in the beauty of the whole."

40

simple
RULE
9

LAW OF BALANCE

"Every building should be so composed that the parts of it on either side of an imaginary line expressed in some manner in the design, shall be of apparently equal weight; and, the central portion, to be successful, must be strongly dominant."

~ Talbot Hamlin

Hamlin, Talbot Faulkner (1889-1956) was an architect, author, architectural historian and educator, who wrote influential books on architectural design. He created the Avery Architectural Index while at Columbia University.

LAW OF BALANCE

Palladio villa

"The most simple application of this law is seen in symmetrical buildings... Symmetry—the exact correspondence of the two halves of a building— can only exist when a building is in perfect balance.

Symmetrical buildings may themselves be divided into classes, corresponding to several different schemes of design, more or less complex. The simpler schemes are the most universally successful, and it becomes increasingly difficult to manage the whole composition as motives are added, since the increasing complexity makes it difficult for the eye to seize at once the inherent balance, which is such a large element in the beauty of the whole.

The simplest of these symmetrical masses is, of course, the plain rectangular front, with or without a gable. The symmetry is perfect, and hence the balance. The whole, in absolute, easily grasped balance, is reposeful, satisfying and beautiful."

"A second scheme, a shade more complex, consists of a simple rectangular form in the middle, usually, but not always, long and low in effect, with a smaller, but strongly accented form at each end.

Without this additional weight at the corners the building would have had an undistinguished, indecisive air. There would have been always the feeling that there was no reason for the building ending where it did …"

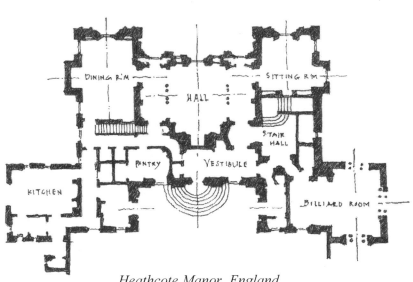

Heathcote Manor, England
Edwin Lutyens

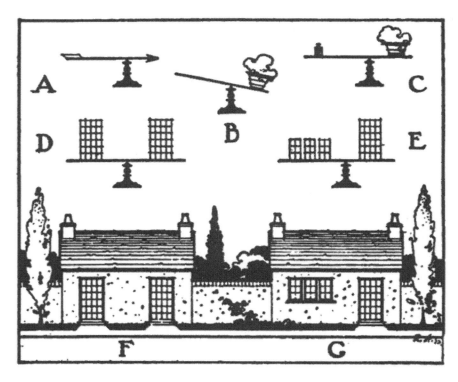

diagrams showing types of balance, imbalance

simple
RULE
10

LAW OF LEVERAGE

"Masses on one side of an interesting pivotal feature must have counterbalancing masses on the other side; shapes and positions of the masses themselves affect the balance."

~ Talbot Hamlin

L-shaped house with center entry; chimney balancing left side, arched window balancing composition on the right

LAW OF LEVERAGE

"First, a heavy member close to that interesting feature which expresses the centre of balance—the pivot, as it were—will counterbalance and be balanced by a long, low, lighter member further from that point.

Secondly, the shapes and positions of the masses themselves affect the balance. A member that projects forward always seems heavier than a receding member.

The best place on an "L" type building for the centre of interest is on the long side, near the angle, (the projecting wing, nearer the eye, seems heavier than the rest, requires a longer portion to balance it.)"

a.   b.

Fig. a.
A balanced composition, where entry porch is the pivotal point of interest,
with taller mass on the left balanced by a wider mass on the right.
Fig b.
An unbalanced composition, where entry porch is the pivotal point of interest,
but both the taller mass and wider mass are both left of the main focus.

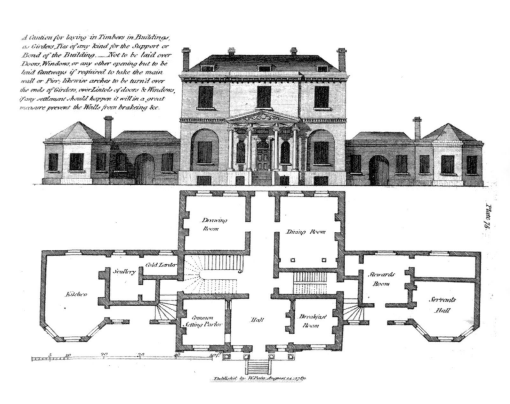

A Caution for laying in Timbers in Buildings, as Girders, Ties of any kind for the Support or Bond of the Building. Not to be laid over Doors, Windows, or any other opening but to be laid Gantways if required to take the main wall or Pier, likewise arches to be turn'd over the ends of Girders, over Lintels of doors & Windows, if any settlement should happen it will in a great measure prevent the Walls from braking &c.

William Pain Builder Handbook

48

simple

11

AXES

"Every building should be so composed that the parts of it on either side of an imaginary line expressed in some manner in the design, shall be of apparently equal weight; and, the central portion, to be successful, must be strongly dominant."

~ Talbot Hamlin

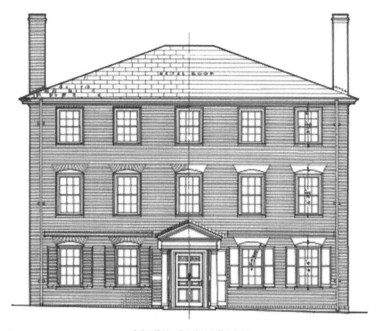

· SOUTH · ELEVATION ·

Longfellow House, Cambridge
"Hundreds of colonial houses, such as the Longfellow house in Cambridge, …where the central, dominant portion suggests the welcome of the entrance, and the less dominant portions on either side the various rooms to which the entrance leads. … the danger is that the side portions shall become unduly important, through size, or decorative treatment, so that the effect of the centre is lost, and again confusion results."

~ Talbot Hamlin

AXES

" The imaginary lines upon which and around which the plan is built, are called axes. There are also auxiliary axes for the minor features of the plan.

The simplest way of recognizing the law of balance in architecture is to dispose symmetrically the elements of plan and elevation on either side of axial lines.

The main axis should pass through the center of the mass and should result in a well-balanced and symmetrical arrangement of dominant parts."

~Abraham Benton Greenberg, Charles Burton Howe
Architectural Drafting

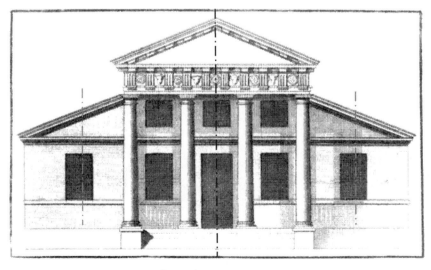

formal symmetry

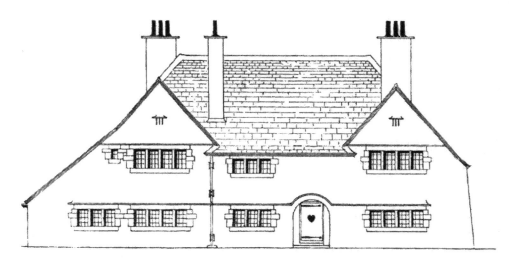

The Orchards CFA Voysey

simple
RULE

12

ASYMMETRY

Balance in Asymmetry: "the axis of balance must be expressed in some way, by door, or balcony, or porch, or some interesting feature. This, perhaps, is the most important point of all. If the axis of balance is so expressed by such a feature of the building, the eye will be drawn to it at once, and, resting on it, will feel that the mass of building on each side is approximately equal. "

~ Talbot Hamlin

ASYMMETRY

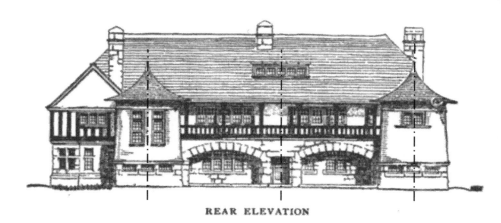

REAR ELEVATION

Where "the lack of symmetry is in certain details, rather than in scheme… if well carried out is always successful … but balance and beauty result only when the mass of the two unsymmetrical parts is kept almost the same."

~ Talbot Hamlin
The Enjoyment of Architecture

ASYMMETRY

solid vertical gable wing on right, balanced by open horizontal porch on left, common base stone transitions grade change, ties the whole composition together

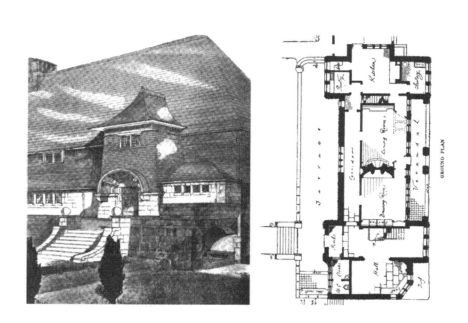

asymmetrical compositions are not arbitrary, but rather tend toward symmetry, using asymmetrical parts

ASYMMETRY

"The balance of inclinations is felt more than the balance of shapes."

~ Dr. Denmon Ross in *The Aesthetic Attitude (1920)*

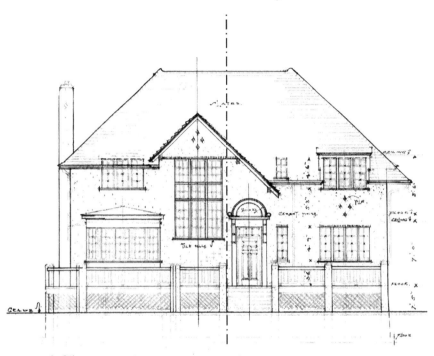

: FRONT . ELEVATION :

asymmetrical but balanced composition:
doorway balanced by adjacent window in gable, curved bay window
balanced by composition of four grouped and one single window,
chimney offset with roof overhang and raised shed dormer

MOULDING ASSEMBLY

"A profile is an assemblage of essential parts and mouldings."

MOULDINGS

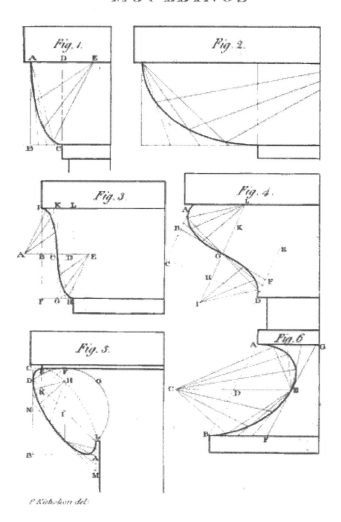

Grecian mouldings

simple
RULE

13

MOULDING ASSEMBLY

Proper Use of Mouldings:
"That profile produces the happiest effect which is composed of but few members, varied in form and size, and arranged so that the plane and the curved surfaces succeed each other alternately."

~ Robert Griffith Hatfield

Hatfield, Robert Griffith, (1815-1879) Architect, Late Fellow of the AIA, Member of The American Society Of Civil Engineers, wrote a builder guide *The American House-Carpenter,* published in 1844.

MOULDING ASSEMBLY

"A profile is an assemblage of essential parts and mouldings"

"… each one is common to all; and although each has its appropriate use, yet it is by no means confided to any certain position in an assemblage of mouldings.

The use of the **fillet** is to bind the parts, as also that of the **astragal** and **torus**, which resemble ropes.

The **ovolo** and **cyma-reversa** are strong at their upper extremities, and are therefore used to support projecting parts above them.

The quick turnings of the **ovolo** and **cyma-reversa**, in particular, when exposed to a bright sun, cause those narrow, well-defined streaks of light, which give life and splendour to the whole.

The **cyma-recta** and **cavetto**, being weak at their upper extremities, are not used as supporters, but are placed uppermost to cover and shelter the other parts.

The **scotia** is introduced in the base of a column, to separate the upper and lower **torus**, and to produce a pleasing variety and relief.

The form of the **bead**, and that of the **torus**, is the same; the reasons for giving distinct names to them are, that

the **torus**, in every order, is always considerably larger than the **bead**, and is placed among the base mouldings, whereas

the **bead** is never placed there, but on the capital or entablature;

the **torus**, also, is never carved, whereas the **bead** is; and while the **torus** among the Greeks is frequently elliptical in its form, the **bead** retains its circular shape.

While the **scotia** is the reverse of the **torus**, the **cavetto** is the reverse of the **ovolo**, and the **cymarecta** and **cyma-reversa** are combinations of the **ovolo** and **cavetto**."

"That profile produces the happiest effect which is composed of but few members, varied in form and size, and arranged so that the plane and the curved surfaces succeed each other alternately."
~ Robert Griffith Hatfield

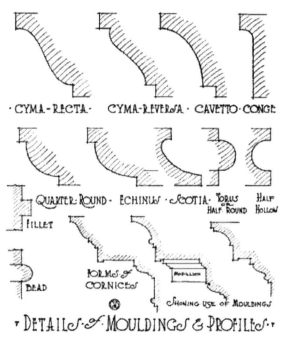

~ George W. Seaman,
Progressive Steps in Architectural Drawing 1919

MOULDINGS ASSEMBLY

Some of the terms are derived thus:

Fillet   from the French word *fil*, thread.

Astragal   from *astragals*, a bone of the heel—or the curvature of the heel.

Bead   because this moulding, when properly carved, resembles a string of beads.

Torus   or *tore*, the Greek for rope, which it resembles, when on the base of a column.

Scotia   from *shotia*, [shadow] darkness, because of the strong shadow which its depth produces, and which is increased by the projection of the torus above it.

Ovolo   from *ovum*, an egg, which this member resembles, when carved, as in the Ionic capital.

Cavetto   from *cavus*, [cave] hollow.

Cymatium   from *kumaton*, a wave.

"Roman mouldings are composed of parts of circles, and have, therefore, less beauty of form than the Grecian [which are composed of ovals]." ~ Robert Griffith Hatfield

"A moulding is so called, because of its being of the same determinate shape along its whole length, as though the whole of it had been cast in the same mould or form."

~ Robert Griffith Hatfield
The American House-Carpenter 1844

Mouldings or Members

Fillet, List, Listel, Reglet, Annulet, or Bandelette

Baguette, or Astragal

Tore, or Baton

Scotia, Canal, Trochilus

Ovolo, Quarter round Echinus, Boultin & inverted erect   Lesbian Astragal

Cavetto, Semi canal, Conge, and Doric Cymatium

Gorge

Ogee, or Talon inverted erect

Cymatium, Cyma, Gula, Doucine, & Gorge inverted erect

Corona, Larmier, Drip, & Mouchette

Plafond, & Soffito

Baguette, with Ribband   Roses

Chaplet, with Flowers, Paternost, Beads

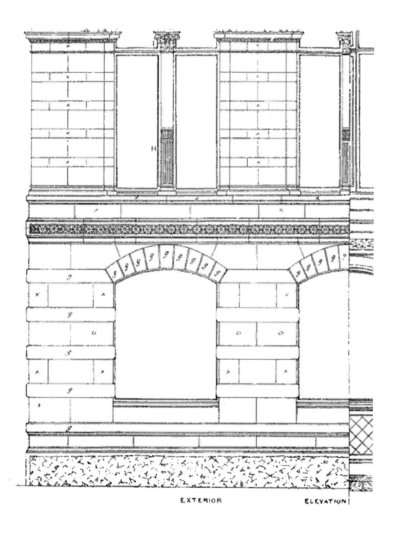

EXTERIOR   ELEVATION

simple
RULE

14

UNIT SIZE TO BUILDING SCALE

"…the whole and each particular member should be a multiple of some simple unit"

~ Owen Jones

Jones, Owen (1809–1874) was an English-born Welsh architect, one of the most influential design theorists of the 19th century. His theories on flat patterning, ornament and color theory originated with detailed study of Islamic art.

UNIT SIZE TO BUILDING SCALE

"Architectural size is measured in terms of the human figure. It would be impracticable, however, to adhere closely to this unit, especially in sculptural decoration of buildings.

It is necessary to increase such figures to avoid the appearance of diminution, due to juxtaposition with elements that must inevitably partake of unusual dimensions.

The actual size of units must harmonize with the scale of the building. Very large stones appear out of place on a small cottage, or very small stones on a large building.

Especially on the interior, members of great strength must be considerably masked, to obviate their crushing effect.

In short, 'absolute frankness' would be as disastrous in architectural design as in everyday life."

~ George A. Hool, Nathan C. Johnson,
Handbook of Building Construction: Data for Architects (1920)

Hool, George Albert (1883-1952?) author of books on architecture and engineering, with emphasis on concrete and long span structures.

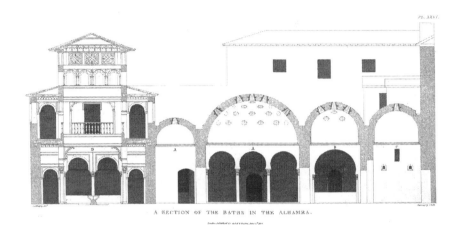

A SECTION OF THE BATHS IN THE ALHAMBRA.

Alhambra courtyard, Granada Spain

"In the matter of scale,
small units may be made to
increase the apparent size
of a building, or large ones
to diminish it."

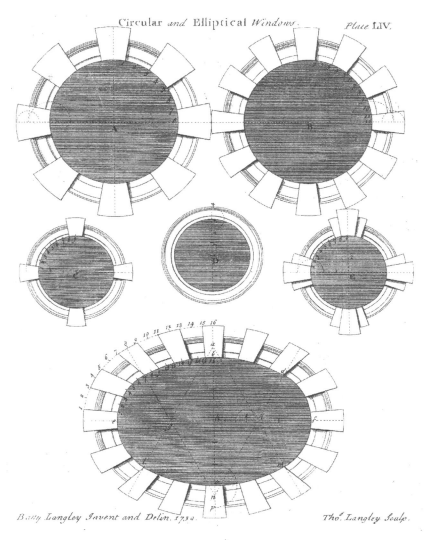

Circular and Elliptical Windows. Plate LIV.

Batty Langley Invent and Delin. 1739. Tho.º Langley Sculp.

Batty Langley
The City and Country Builder's and Workman's Treasury of Designs

Langley, Batty (1696 –1751) was an English garden designer, and prolific writer on architecture and garden design. As a prominent Freemason, his engravings were referenced in important buildings, such as Mount Vernon.

simple
RULE
15

SCALE IN DETAILING

"as scale diminishes, detail must be simplified"

~John Vredenburgh Van Pelt

Van Pelt, John Vredenburgh (1874 – 1962) was an architectural historian, author, and American architect active in early to mid-twentieth-century New York City.

SCALE IN DETAILING

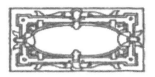

panels, aesthetically adjusted to fit to a specific dimension

"Suppose several panels, of individual lengths are to form a frieze. In the first of these panels we introduce certain elements making a complete design; in the second we must not attempt to enlarge these elements to fill the greater space, [but instead]...**adding new elements of like character** to complete the panel. In the smaller panels some of the elements are merely left out."

"It becomes plain why mechanical reductions and enlargements are so bad. In such reductions the same amount of detail is crowded into a smaller space." [Or not enough detail is stretched to fit a larger one.]

why mechanical reductions and enlargements adjusted to fit to a specific dimension are so bad

If two Greek frets, of different dimensions, are used in the same composition the smaller must be the simpler... If dentals are indicated in a main cornice they should be omitted from a smaller one."

A Discussion of Composition, Especially as Applied to Architecture
~John Vredenburgh Van Pelt

SCALE IN DETAILING

Conversely, "enlarged figures must have more detail given them; the hem of a robe, treated with brocaded designs, perhaps, or the shield of a warrior, embossed with bas-reliefs...

If two Greek frets, of different dimensions, are used in the same composition the smaller must be the simpler...

If dentals are indicated in a main cornice they should be omitted from a smaller one."

~ Van Pelt

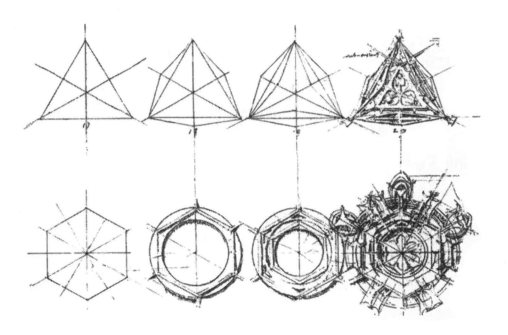

Louis Sullivan, Study of Progressive Detail in Geometric Forms

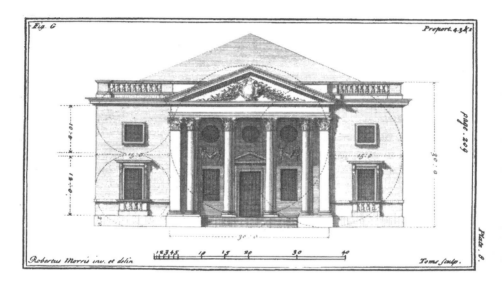

~ Robert Morris
Elevation Study of Proportions

simple
RULE

16

PROPORTION

"Proportion is that agreeable
harmony between the several parts
of a building, which is the result of
a just and regular agreement of
them with each other; the height
to the width, this to the length,
and each of these to the whole."

~ Marcus Vitruvius Pollio

PROPORTION

"in all perfect works, each part should be some aliquot part of the whole"

~ Marcus Vitruvius Pollio

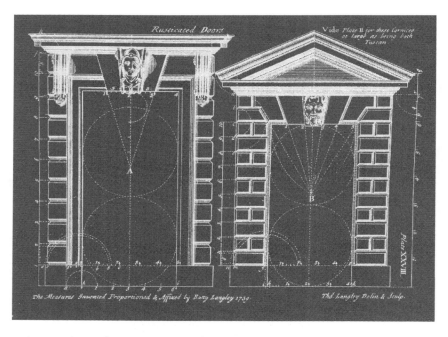

a just and regular agreement of them with each other; the height to the width, this to the length, and each of these to the whole

aliquot:
describing a number that will divide another number without a remainder   (3:6, 4:12, 5:20)

"just and regular agreement of the parts of a building with each other... the measures necessarily used in all buildings and other works, are derived from the members of the human body, as the digit, the palm, the foot, the cubit, and that these form a perfect number......numbers had their origin from the human body, and proportion is the result of a due adjustment of the different parts to each other, and to the whole, they are especially to be commended, who...so arrange the parts that the whole may harmonize in their proportions and symmetry."

traditional system for proportioning of a house overall, and in the distribution of parts and in the detailing

PROPORTION

The ancients considered 10 a perfect number,

because the fingers are ten in number, and the palm is derived from them, and from the palm is derived the foot. ...mathematicians, on the other hand, contend for the perfection of the number 6, because, according to their reasoning, its divisors equal its number: for a sixth part is one, a third two, a half three, two-thirds four, ... as the foot is the sixth part of a man's height, [mathematicians] contend, that this number, namely six, the number of feet in height, is perfect: the cubit, also, being six palms, consequently consists of twenty-four digits. ... finding the numbers six and ten perfect, they added them together, and formed sixteen, a still more perfect number. The foot measure gave rise to this, for subtracting two palms from the cubit, four remains, which is the length of a foot; and as each palm contains four digits, the foot will consequently contain sixteen.

~ Marcus Vitruvius Pollio
De Architectura, Book I

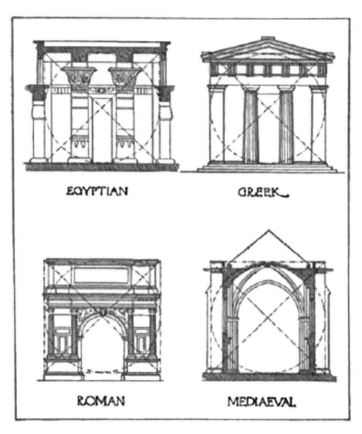

EGYPTIAN   GREEK

ROMAN   MEDIAEVAL

~ John Beverley Robinson, *Architectural Composition*

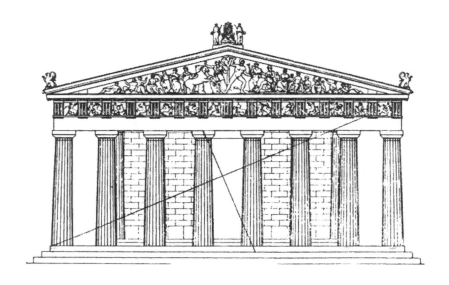

Parthenon, Athens Greece
distribution of parts according to arithmetical proportion; with
diagonal relationships consistent, here the smaller spacing is
perpendicular to the overall diagonal

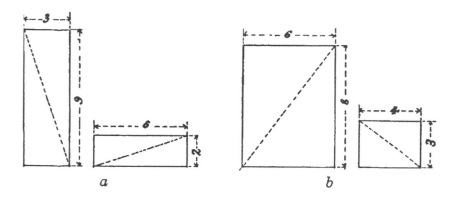

simple

RULE

17

TWO TYPES OF RATIOS

"We shall therefore borrow all our Rules for the Finishing our Proportions, from the Musicians, who are the greatest Masters of this Sort of Numbers, and from those Things wherein Nature shows herself most excellent and compleat."

~ Leon Battista Alberti

Alberti, Leon Battista (1404 –1472) was an Italian architect, author, artist, poet, priest, linguist, philosopher, cryptographer and general Renaissance humanist polymath. *De Re Aedificatoria* a treatise on architecture, using as its basis the work of Vitruvius and influenced by the archaeological remains of Rome.

TWO TYPES OF RATIOS

"The divisions of the stretched string that produce harmonious musical notes have been known from antiquity for their simplicity.

They are these: 1-2, 8-15, 3-5, 2-3, 3-4, 4-5, 8-9.

If these ratios be regarded as the sides of rectangles, each series will give us a succession of rectangles less and less elongated— more and more approaching a square, each one nearly similar to its neighbors, the next larger and the next smaller, but totally different from the extremes either way… yet all connected by a regular system."

Line: *Musical*   1:2::2:4

Point: *Arithmetical*   1:2::2:3

Robinson, John Beverley (1853 - 1923) architect, author of several articles and books on the subject of architecture. Graduate of Columbia University, Robinson served as professor in charge the School of Architecture of Washington University in St. Louis, Missouri.

TWO TYPES OF RATIOS

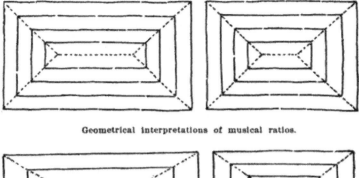

Geometrical interpretations of musical ratios.

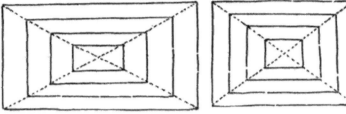

Geometrical interpretations of arithmetical ratios.

"Draw a straight line of a certain length. From the extremities draw diagonals of 45 degrees. ... or, instead of starting with a line, we start with a point, and draw our diagonals at any angle.

The resulting rectangles are **all of the same character**, all elongated or all shortened; while in [the musical ratios] there is a general similarity with continual variation.

Arithmetically this means a series of ratios related to each other by a different connection than that of equality... the ratio proceeding by addition instead of multiplication."

~ John Beverley Robinson
Principles Of Architectural Composition (1899)

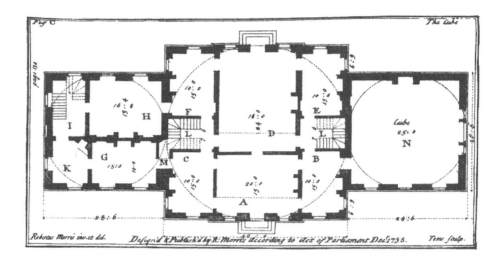

Robert Morris
Proportion Study of Floor Plan

simple
RULE

18

HARMONIOUS ROOM
PROPORTIONS

"seven sets of the most beautiful and harmonious proportions to be used in the construction of rooms"

~ Andrea Palladio

Palladio, Andrea (1508 –1580) an Italian architect, influenced by Roman and Greek architecture. Heavily influenced by writings of Vitruvius, Palladio summarized his own architectural philosophy in a treatise, *The Four Books of Architecture*. The Palladian Villa is one of the most recognized and copied buildings in the history of Western architecture, and is the inspiration for the classical, symmetrical, geometrical "Palladian" style of architecture.

HARMONIOUS ROOM PROPORTIONS

Andrea Palladio proposed seven ideal room..."measurements which reflected musical consonances."

1. Circular	1
2. Square	1:1
3. The diagonal of the square	1:1.414...
4. A square plus a third	3:4
5. A square plus a half	2:3
6. A square plus two-thirds	3:5
7. Double square	1:2

~ Andrea Palladio
The Four Books of Architecture, 1570

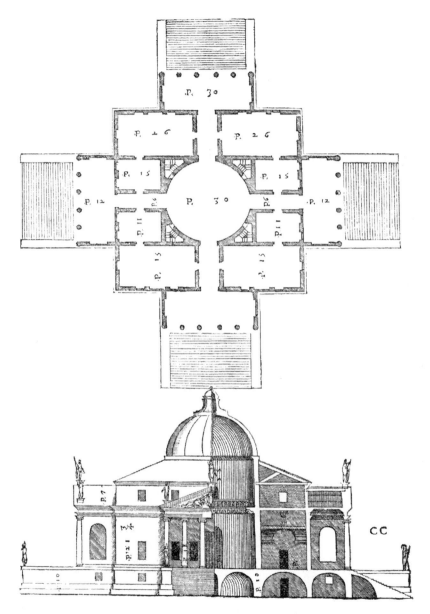

Andrea Palladio, Villa Rotunda

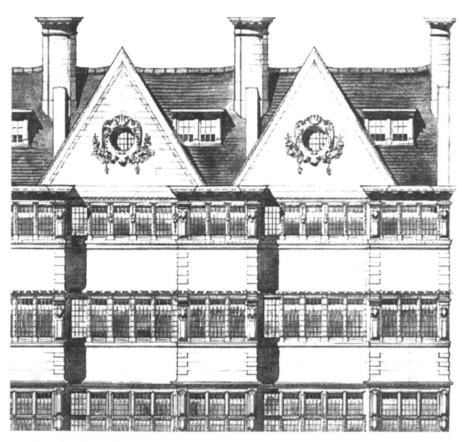

bands of windows broken up with projected bays in a 3-5-3 repetition,
offset chimney and dormer window above break up symmetrical
sameness of horizontal banding below

simple
RULE
19

SIMILARITY & REPETITION

"Similarity enlivened by difference, variety restrained by unity, may be found in all the arrangements of light and shade, form, and colour, and sound, which are most pleasing to the eye and to the ear."

~ John Addington Symonds

"Repetition is agreeable, not only if the thing is pleasant in itself, and before the repetition palls, but also through the recognition of the feeling, as being like what had been felt before.

That enjoyment should accrue from the perception of similarities is scarcely less important than the gratification of variety, because we thus learn to classify the objects of our knowledge. But mere likeness without difference becomes distasteful sameness or dull uniformity,—just as mere variety without likeness would be intolerable; for in this case there would be a number of insulated experiences without any connection."

It is similarity which constitutes the pleasure derived from imitation, and not merely the pleasure of witnessing the successful production of likeness; for, even if the imitation is accidental, the spectator is pleased, as in the fortuitous resemblances occasionally seen in nature—as of stones which have some resemblances to plants, …

mere likeness without difference becomes

distasteful sameness

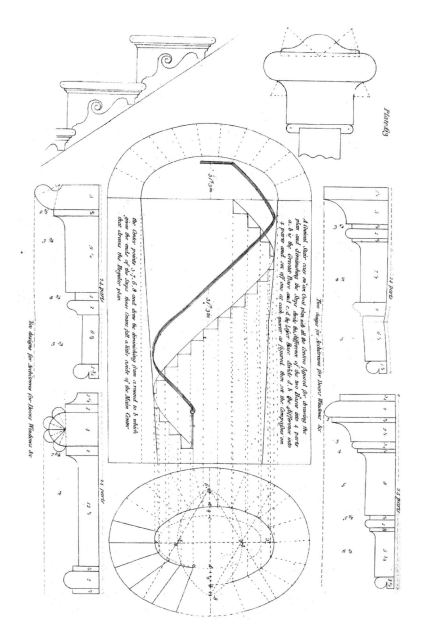

plate from early builders handbook

simple
RULE
20

GRACE

"the secret of graceful action is that the symmetry is preserved through all the varieties of position"

~William Hogarth

Grace is found in postures implying minimal effort or resistant force:

"...we commonly, and perhaps unavoidably, regard all objects under a certain anthropomorphic aspect... The stiff branch of an oak tree standing out at right angles to the trunk, gives us a vague notion of great force expended to keep it in that position; and we call it ungraceful, under the same feeling that we call the holding out an arm at right angles to the body ungraceful. Conversely, the lax drooping boughs of a weeping-willow are vaguely associated with limbs in *attitudes requiring little effort* to maintain them; and the term graceful, by which we describe these, we apply by metaphor to the boughs of the willow."

~ Herbert Spenser, *Gracefulness* (1852)

"Grace—that is, beauty in motion and attitude—is a striking illustration of the union of the two principles of *similarity* and *variety*... in works of architecture, we found lines, angles, and curves, associated in a manner delightful to the sense of symmetry."

~William Hogarth, *Analysis of Beauty*

GRACE

"The perception of grace in inanimate objects differs only slightly from that of the graceful impression made by moving objects... the pleasure of graceful lines and forms is transmitted by the manner in which the lines of the object suggest movement to the observer."

~ Herbert Sidney Langfeld, *The Aesthetic Attitude* (1920)

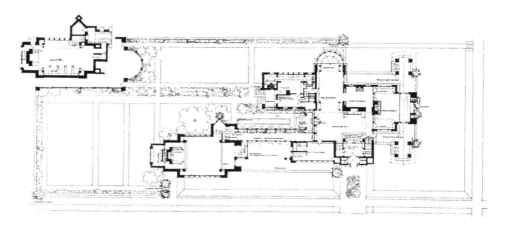

Frank Lloyd Wright Dana House

"grace and perfect proportion require an elongation in some one direction"

~John Ruskin, *Seven Lamps of Architecture*

Ruskin, John (1819 –1900) English art critic of the Victorian era, wrote on many subjects including architecture, particularly Gothic revival. His book Seven Lamps of Architecture covered the moral aspects inseparable from all architecture: sacrifice, truth, power, beauty, life, memory and obedience.

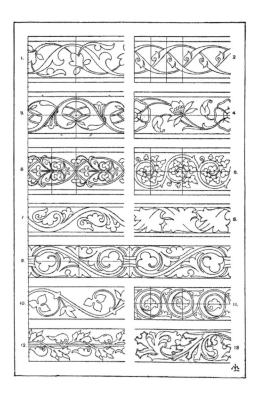

"The eye hath this sort of enjoyment in winding walks, and serpentine rivers, and all sorts of objects... composed principally of ... waving and serpentine lines. [They lead] a wanton kind of chase, and from the pleasure that gives the mind, entitles it to the name of beautiful"

~William Hogarth, *Analysis of Beauty*

RESONANCE

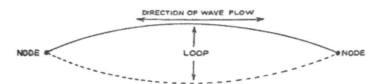

DIRECTION OF WAVE FLOW

NODE

LOOP

NODE

A MUSICAL STRING RESONATING AS A UNIT-WAVE SOUNDS ITS
FUNDAMENTAL FREQUENCY.
NOTE THAT THE FLOW OF ENERGY ALONG THE LENGTH OF THE STANDING-
WAVE IS TRANSFORMED INTO AN ALTERNATING CURRENT FLOWING
AT RIGHT-ANGLES ACROSS THE LOOP AFTER A REDUCTION OF
WAVELENGTH AND VELOCITY AS DETERMINED BY THE LOOP/LENGTH RATIO.

AT THE SAME TIME THAT A STRING RESONATES AS A UNIT,
IT ALSO VIBRATES AS TWO WAVE-UNITS TO SOUND THE
SECOND HARMONIC OVERTONE AT TWICE THE FREQUENCY
OF THE FUNDAMENTAL.

AND AT THE SAME TIME AS A STRING SOUNDS ITS
FUNDAMENTAL FREQUENCY AND ITS SECOND HARMONIC
OVERTONE, IT ALSO RESONATES AS THREE WAVE-UNITS
TO SOUND ITS THIRD HARMONIC OVERTONE AT THREE
TIMES THE FUNDAMENTAL FREQUENCY, AND SO ON TO
INFINITY BY WAY OF THE FOURTH, FIFTH AND SIXTH OVERTONES.

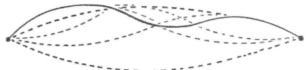

A COMPOUND WAVE IS FORMED BY SUPERIMPOSED HARMONIC OVERTONES.

~ Walter Russell

simple
RULE

21

RESONANCE

"Beauty resonates from intricacies
of serpentine lines, interlaced in
distinct varied quantities, as in
music, from a compound wave
formed by superimposed
harmonic overtones."

~William Hogarth

"interlacing ...in distinct varied quantities is an artful way of preserving as much of intricacy, as is beautiful"

~ William Hogarth, *Analysis of Beauty*

INTERLACE: INTERLACED PATTERNS FROM THE ALHAMBRA, GRANADA, SPAIN

Alhambra, Granada, Spain
Islamic-style interlaced tile patterns, in conjunction with similar carved and painted patterns, generate a music-like energy that resonates throughout the compound

RESONANCE

" that which in music is expressed by means of
harmonious intervals of time and pitch, successively,
after the manner of time, may be translated into
corresponding intervals of architectural void and solid,
height and width "

~ Claude Bragdon, *Beautiful Necessity*

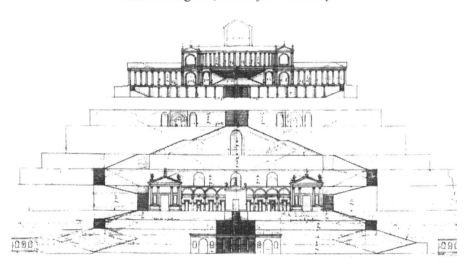

Palladio, Temple Fortuna
traffic flow does not simply march singly up the center of the
composition, but is flanked either side with a gracefully graduated
staircase, that meanders melodically back and forth up the hill in
accordance to a rhythm

Gothic window detail

simple
RULE

22

BRANCHING FORMS IN DECORATION

"Beauty of form is produced by lines growing out one from the other in gradual undulations."

~ Owen Jones

Owen Jones, The Grammar of Ornament (1856)

"In surface decoration all lines should flow out of a perfect stem. Every ornament, however distant, should be traced to its branch and root. All junctions of curved lines with curved or of curved lines with straight should be tangential to each other."

BRANCHING FORMS IN DECORATION

Beauty of form is produced by lines growing out one from the other in gradual undulations; there are no excrescences; nothing could be removed and leave the design equally good or better.

The general forms being first cared for, these should be subdivided and ornamented by general lines; the interstices may then be filled in with ornament, which again may be subdivided and enriched for closer inspection.

Owen Jones, The Grammar of Ornament (1856)

Morris wallpaper design

"Do not introduce any lines or objects which cannot be explained by the structure of the pattern; it is just this logical sequence of form, this growth which looks as if, under the circumstances, it could not have been otherwise, which prevents the eye wearying of the repetition of the pattern."

~ William Morris *Arts and Crafts Essays* (1893)

vertical

Vertical lines add always to slenderness

∴

Horizontal lines increase strength

horizontal

simple
RULE

23

EXPRESSION OF CHARACTER

"There are two principles of composition for elevations — the horizontal and the vertical; one of these must predominate."

~ Thomas L Donaldson, *Arch Maxims*

Donaldson, Thomas Leverton (1795 –1885) was a British architect, notable as a pioneer in architectural education, as a co-founder and President of the Royal Institute of British Architects and a winner of the RIBA Royal Gold Medal. In 1841 he became the first Professor of Architecture at University College London

Front : Elevation

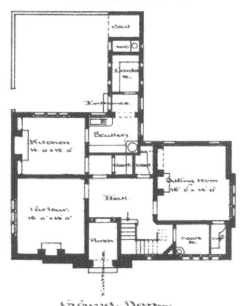

Ground : Floor

subtle verticality initiated by tall roof form, vertical windows, wall expanse, exaggerated chimney

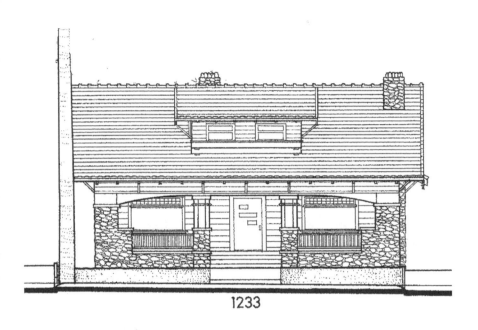

1233

*horizontality reinforced by dormer and windows, flattened arch,
shortened columns, short chimneys*

GROUND PLAN

FIRST FLOOR

Artist's Cottage, (1885)
CFA Voysey Architect

simple

RULE

24

PICTURESQUE

"a principle… of picturesque character [directs] a certain subordination of the various parts of a composition to one predominant feature or group."

Sydney Smirke, Lecture IV

Smirke, Sydney (1798 – 1877) London architect, received the RIBA Royal Gold Medal in 1860, wrote articles for The Civil Engineer and Architect's Journal.

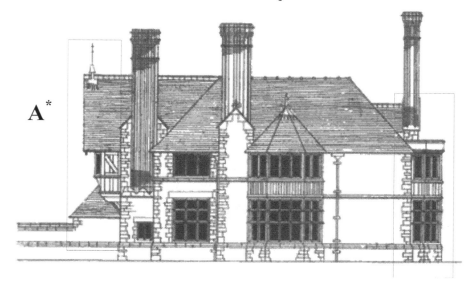

A *

A

element A*, upper bay left, is balanced proportionately with element A, lower bay, on the right.

composition of picturesque asymmetrical elements balanced around a strong central element (the curved bay window and adjacent chimney together establish the central focus).

"In every large composition, whether it be a building, or ...picture, a kind of unity should be preserved by concentrating effect; by giving, not indeed an undue absorbing interest to any one portion of the design, but a decided and clearly marked preponderance to one portion, ... where interest is scattered it is sure to be weakened."

PICTURESQUE

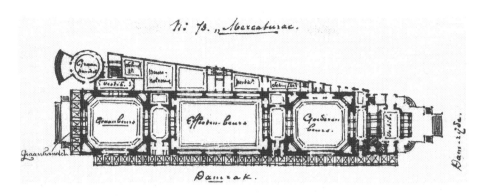

~ Berlage
three central halls establish the central focus for all the adjacent support areas that fill in the odd shaped lot

"Two ideas, therefore, are essential to picturesqueness,—the first, that of sublimity (for pure beauty is not picturesque at all, and becomes so only as the sublime element mixes with it), and the second, the subordinate or parasitical position of that sublimit... whatever characters of line or shade or expression are productive of sublimity, will become productive of picturesqueness... angular and broken lines, vigorous oppositions of light and shadow, and grave, deep, or boldly contrasted color; and all these are in a still higher degree effective, when, by resemblance or association, they remind us of objects on which a true and essential sublimity exists, as of rocks or mountains, or stormy clouds or waves."

John Ruskin, *Seven Lamps of Architecture*

simple
RULE

25

FRANKNESS & DECISIVENESS

"One of the most difficult, yet vital things to accomplish is the delineation of character, in all the practical elements necessary to the building."

~ Sydney Smirke

FRANKNESS & DECISIVENESS

"… good designs are made of parts of different rank, because of different sizes and positions; an agreeable and forceful design must have clear indication of these parts and of their rank.

This indication is made chiefly by block relations of mass, but also by treatment of details such as cornices, belt-courses, door and window casings, chimneys, pilasters, brackets, trellises, waterpipes, and the like."

~ Arthur Bridgman Clark

"All practically required elements should be frankly shown, never hidden through a fear of their not being decorative. This delineation of character cannot be carried too far; and in its finer expression it is one of the most difficult things to accomplish."

~ John Vredenburgh Van Pelt
A Discussion of Composition, Especially as Applied to Architecture

On Lost Wisdom

"Were these invaluable books more generally known and understood, if they did not refine our taste, at present so depraved, they would at least teach us to admire the strength which human reason is capable of exerting, and to be more modest in our pretensions to wisdom; they would silence ignorant declaimers, and stop the immense increase of books on modern philosophy, which are so rapidly hastening to the abyss of forgetfulness, like streams into the ocean from which they originally flowed."

~Thomas Taylor (commenting in regards to the Greek myths)
Hymns of Orpheus 1787

Taylor, Thomas (1758 –1835) was an English philosopher author and expert on ancient mythology, he was the first to translate the complete works of Aristotle and of Plato, as well as the Orphic fragments into English.

THE END

SOURCES

Alberti, Leon Battista, *Ten Books on Architecture, De Re Aedificatoria (1486)*

Brown, Richard, Architect, *Domestic Architecture: Containing a History of the Science (1841)*

Bragdon, Claude F. (1920) *Beautiful Necessity*

Clark, Arthur Bridgman, *Art Principles In House, Furniture, and Village Building, an Exposition of Designing Principles Which Every House Builder... Should Know* (1921)

Donaldson, Thomas L, *Architectural Maxims (1847)*

Greenberg, Abraham Benton, Charles Burton Howe *Architectural Drafting (1913)*

Hamlin, Talbot, *The Enjoyment of Architecture (1921)*

Harris, George, *The Theory of the Arts: or, Art in Relation to Nature, Vol 2 (1869)*

Hatfield, Robert Griffith, *The American House-Carpenter (1844)*

Hogarth, William, *Analysis of Beauty (1753)*

Hool, George A. and Nathan C. Johnson, *Handbook of Building Construction: Data for Architects (1920)*

Jones, Owen, *The Grammar of Ornament (1856)*

Langfeld, Herbert Sidney, *The Aesthetic Attitude (1920)*

Langley, Batty *The City and Country Builder's and Workman's Treasury of Designs (1756)*

Jones, Inigo, William Kent, *Designs of Inigo Jones and others (1735)*

Palladio, Andrea, *The Four Books of Architecture (1570)*

Pope, Alexander, *The Works of Alexander Pope (1754)*

Robinson, John Beverley, *Principles Of Architectural Composition (1899)*

SOURCES

Ruskin, John *Seven Lamps of Architecture (1849)*

Seaman, George W., *Progressive Steps in Architectural Drawing (1919)*

Smirke, Sydney *On Architecture At The Royal Academy, Lecture I (1877)*

Spenser, Herbert, *Gracefulness (1852)*

Stratton, Arthur, *Elements of Form & Design in Classic Architecture (1925)*

Taylor, Thomas, *Hymns of Orpheus (1787)*

Vitruvius Pollio, Marcus, *De Architectura, Book I (1486);*

The Architecture of Marcus Vitruvius Pollio, English tr. by J. Gwilt (1874)

Vredenburgh Van Pelt, John, *A Discussion of Composition, Especially as Applied to Architecture (1902)*

William Morris, *Arts and Crafts Essays (1893)*

BIOGRAPHIES

Alberti, Leon Battista (1404 –1472) was an Italian architect, author, artist, poet, priest, linguist, philosopher, cryptographer and general Renaissance humanist polymath. *De Re Aedificatoria* a treatise on architecture, using as its basis the work of Vitruvius and influenced by the archaeological remains of Rome.

Brown, Richard, Architect (1800s) English architect, author of domestic architectural pattern books

Bragdon, Claude Fayette, (1866-1948) New York architect, writer and Theosophist, like Frank Lloyd Wright, believed an "organic architecture" based on nature was an important counter to industrial focus of society

Clark, Arthur Bridgman (1866-1948) was an architect and professor of art at Stanford. He wrote several books including texts on perspective, house design, and community planning.

Donaldson, Thomas Leverton (1795 –1885) was a British architect, notable as a pioneer in architectural education, as a co-founder and President of the Royal Institute of British Architects and a winner of the RIBA Royal Gold Medal. In 1841 he became the first Professor of Architecture at University College London

Greenberg, Abraham Benton (1883-), BA Inspector and Draftsman Supervisor, with Charles Burton Howe (1870-) wrote technical series for vocational and industrial schools, published by J. Wiley & Sons, inc, New York, NY

Hamlin, Talbot Faulkner (1889-1956) was an architect, author, architectural historian and educator, who wrote influential books on architectural design. He created the Avery Architectural Index while at Columbia University.

Harris, George, (1809-1890) English barrister and judge with strong interests in anthropology and psychology published a two-volume treatise titled *A Philosophical Treatise on the Nature and Constitution of Man.* Many theories were novel, but he also utilized medieval principles and terminology.

Hatfield, Robert Griffith, *The American House-Carpenter (1844)* Hatfield (1815-1879) Architect, Late Fellow of the AIA, Member of The American Society Of Civil Engineers

Hogarth, William (1697 –1764) was an English painter, printmaker, pictorial satirist, social critic, and editorial cartoonist credited with pioneering western sequential art. He published his ideas of artistic design in his book *The Analysis of Beauty*, where he professed to define the principles of beauty and grace

Hool, George Albert (1883- 1952?) was an author of books on architecture and engineering, with emphasis on concrete and long span structures.

Jones, Inigo (1573 –1652) was the first significant British architect to employ Vitruvian rules of proportion and symmetry and Palladio's design in his building and stage designs. He annotated Palladio's *Quattro Libri dell' Architecttura.*

Jones, Owen (1809 –1874) was an English-born Welsh architect and one of the most influential design theorists of the nineteenth century. His theories on flat patterning, ornament and color originated with a detailed study of Islamic art.

Langfeld, Herbert Sidney (1879-1958) German psychologist, believed aesthetics should be pragmatic, and that the perception of beauty is one of the most useful of man's experiences.

Langley, Batty (1696 –1751) was an English garden designer, and prolific writer on architecture and garden design. As a prominent Freemason, his engravings were referenced in important buildings, such as Mount Vernon.

Latrobe, Benjamin Henry Boneval (1764 –1820) was a British neoclassical architect who immigrated to the United States and is best known for his design of the United States Capitol. Latrobe was one of the first formally-trained, professional architects in the United States, drawing influences from his travels in Italy, as well as Neoclassical architects such as Claude Nicolas Ledoux.

Morris, William (1834 – 1896) was an English artist, poet, writer, and textile designer. A founder of the Society for the Protection of Ancient Buildings, and known for his role in the English Arts and Crafts Movement, Morris worked to revive traditional textile arts and methods of production, an to reinstate decoration as one of the fine arts.

Palladio, Andrea (1508 –1580) an Italian architect, influenced by Roman and Greek architecture. Heavily influenced by writings of Vitruvius, Palladio summarized his own architectural philosophy in a treatise, *The Four Books of Architecture.* The Palladian Villa is one of the most recognized and copied buildings in the history of Western architecture, and is the inspiration for the classical, symmetrical, geometrical "Palladian" style of architecture.

Pope, Alexander ( ) know for writing Augustan poetry, he used similar principles as an inspiration for landscape design. He established the *genius loci* an important principle in garden and landscape design, which later influenced architects as well.

Robertson, Sir Howard Morley (1888 –1963) was an American-born British architect, President of the Royal Institute of British Architects and a Royal Academician. Authored several books on architectural composition.

Robinson, John Beverley (1853 - 1923) architect, author of several articles and books on the subject of architecture and composition. Graduate of Columbia University, Robinson served as professor in charge the School of Architecture of Washington University in St. Louis, Missouri.

Ruskin, John (1819 –1900) English art critic of the Victorian era, wrote on many subjects including architecture, particularly Gothic revival. His book Seven Lamps of Architecture covered the moral aspects inseparable from all architecture: sacrifice, truth, power, beauty, life, memory and obedience.

Seaman, George W. (1800s) Instructor in Architecture, School of Industrial Arts, Trenton, New Jersey. A practicing architect and writer of a textbook that developed an explanatory system of draftsmanship, to act as "a guide to the young student-draughtsman."

Smirke, Sydney (1798 – 1877) London architect, received the RIBA Royal Gold Medal in 1860

Spenser, Herbert (1820 –1903) was an English philosopher, biologist, anthropologist, sociologist, political theorist of the Victorian era. Best know for his theory on 'first principles.'

Symonds, John Addington (1840 –1893) was an English poet, and literary critic, he was known for his cultural history of Italian Renaissance.

Taylor, Thomas (1758 –1835) was an English philosopher author and expert on ancient mythology, he was the first to translate the complete works of Aristotle and of Plato, as well as the Orphic fragments into English.

Vitruvius Pollio, Marcus, (c80 BC- c15 BC) wrote *De Architectura,* the first and most famous treatises on architecture. Based on Greek architecture, the ten books codified the theories guiding Roman architecture of his time. He described a geometric relationship between nature, architecture and the body of man, which was the basis of the famous DaVinci drawing of the Renaissance man inscribed in a circle and square.

Voysey, Charles Francis Annesley (1857–1941) was a renowned English architect of a number of notable country houses, and designed furniture and textiles in a simple Arts and Crafts style. He was one of the first people to understand and appreciate the significance of industrial design.

Van Pelt, John Vredenburgh (1874 – 1962) was an architectural historian, author, and American architect active in early to mid-twentieth-century New York City.

"The idea that a house must be large in order to be well built, is altogether of modern growth, and is parallel with the idea, that no picture can be historical, except of a size admitting figures larger than life."

John Ruskin, *Seven Lamps of Architecture*

ABOUT THE AUTHOR

Shannon Scarlett wondered even as a child what made one place beautiful and another not. She asked why was there a difference in quality between newer houses and neighborhoods and their older counterparts. While this was not her sole focus when she headed off to architecture school, she did expect to find answers to some of her questions. Unfortunately, the problem seemed to be more complex than expected. No one seemed to really know, or particularly care why the suburbs were failing architecturally.

Though swamped by 'real world' issues of professional life, the issue haunted her subconsciously. After many years in residential practice, helping individual homeowners create homes that were both functional and expressive of their lifestyle, she witnessed firsthand the limits on the individual architect to influence the broader suburban landscape.

Like it or not, the architectural profession abandoned the typical suburban house to focus on custom homes, and suburbia is now substantially the domain of contractors. The problem is that most builders have very little training in or understanding of design. Yes, they are successfully building economical new homes that meet the functional needs of modern life, but its not enough.

The great challenge for architects and builders alike lies in aesthetics and significance: how to craft the character, and add the deeper levels of meaning we find in the typical 1920s bungalow, old Victorian, or even simple traditional farmhouses...

To assist builders in regaining some of the lost building wisdom and to obtain a better understanding of the earlier building processes—how builders were able to capture vitality in the forms, spaces and details of these homes, and keep them suitable to the area and period—Shannon thought old resources must exist that could begin to answers questions on the *art* of building.

She began to look into the ways buildings were made in the past. Wherever possible she sought out information at its source—old carpenters manuals, art composition guides and the scientific literature from the 17th, to 20th century—instead of referring to modern interpretations of the practices, techniques and intent of old building traditions.

What became clear was that the old systems were deeply layered in meaning, yet simple in their use and application. The artisans' ritualistic construction practices, crafted products, and built environment, were all intertwined, and were always designed to align most favorably with the patterns and processes they observed in nature. For this book she has focused primarily on the rules of simplicity and order.

The concepts reintroduced here are often fragmented and imprecise, but the intent is to provoke a different kind of traditional thinking that, when rid of outdated stylistic baggage, can develop into a new kind of contemporary house that positively influences the way we dwell in the future, at home, as good neighbors and as responsible global citizens.

The goal is that additional volumes will follow, but in the meantime, for more Simple Rules and illustrations as they are collected, check out the blog at

www.scarlettarchitects.com/simplerules

Note from Author:
Thank you reading Simple Rules. There is also a kindle version as well, if you find that easier to use. amzn.to/14e0KVA
I really hope you learned something new from this book! If so, it would mean a lot if you could take two minutes to log onto Amazon to rate it and give me a short review!

Thanks again,
Shannon

Made in the USA
Middletown, DE
16 March 2017